Sick Jokes

What's the last thing to go through a bug's mind when he hits a car's windscreen?

HIS BUM!

with Glen Singleton

Crazy Book of Sick Jokes
First published in 2003 by Hinkler Books Pty Ltd
17–23 Redwood Drive
Dingley VIC 3172 Australia
www.hinklerbooks.com

ISBN: 1865156906

Cover designer: Peter Tovey Studios
Editor: Rose Inserra
Typesetting: Midland Typesetters
Printed and bound in Australia

Crazy Book of Sick Jokes

What's green, sticky and
smells like eucalyptus?

Koala vomit.

What is the difference between
broccoli and bogies?

Kids don't like to eat broccoli!

Why did Piglet look in the toilet?

He was looking for Pooh.

What's the last thing that goes through a bug's mind when he hits a car windscreen?

His bottom.

Why do little brothers chew with their mouths full?

Flies have got to live somewhere.

What do you get if you sit under a cow?

A pat on the head.

What is the soft stuff
between sharks' teeth?

Slow swimmers.

Mummy, Mummy, can I lick the bowl?

No! You'll have to flush like everyone else.

What's a sick joke?

Something that comes up in conversation.

Who is the best dancer at a monster party?

The Boogie Man!

What's the difference between
a maggot and a cockroach?

*Cockroaches crunch more
when you eat them.*

'**I** just got a bunch of flowers for my wife.'

'*Great swap.*'

What do you give a sick elephant?

A very big paper bag.

What's brown and sounds like a bell?

Dung.

Why do service stations always
lock their toilets?

They are afraid someone might clean them.

What do you do if your nose goes on strike?

Picket.

What does a boy monster do when a girl monster rolls her eyes at him?

He rolls them back to her.

Little Monster: 'I hate my teacher's guts!'

Mum Monster: 'Then just eat around them!'

Little Monster: 'Should I eat my
fries with my fingers?'

*Mum Monster: 'No, you should
eat them separately!'*

Mum, everyone at school
calls me a werewolf.

Shut up and comb your face.

How does a monster count to thirteen?

On his fingers.

Mother vampire to son: 'Hurry up and eat your breakfast before it clots.'

What looks like Blu-Tak, feels like Blu-Tak, tastes like Blu-Tak, but isn't Blu-Tak?

Smurf poo.

What's old, wrinkled and hangs out your jocks?

Your Grandma.

How can you tell when a moth farts?

He flies straight for a second.

How do you make a hankie dance?

Put some boogie into it.

What has two grey legs and two brown legs?

An elephant with diarrhoea.

What makes you seasick?

Your little brother's vomit.

What are hundreds and thousands?

Smartie poo.

What's another name for a snail?

A booger with a crash helmet.

What's yellow and smells of bananas?

Monkey vomit.

What's green and red and goes at 120 kph?

A frog in a blender.

What has fifty legs and can't walk?

Half a centipede.

'**D**addy, can I have another
glass of water, please?'

*'Okay, but that's the twelfth one
I've given you tonight.'*

'Yes I know, but the baby's
bedroom is still on fire.'

'**C**an I go swimming now, Mum?'
asked the child.

*'No – there are sharks at this beach,'
said his mother.*

'Dad's swimming!'

'Yes, he's got a million dollars' life insurance.'

What's the difference between school
lunches and a pile of slugs?

School lunches are on plates.

Did you hear about the two fat
men who ran a marathon?

*One ran in short bursts,
the other ran in burst shorts.*

What do nudists like to eat best?

Skinless sausages.

A woman woke her husband
in the middle of the night.

'There's a burglar in the kitchen eating the cake I made this morning!' she said.

'Who should I call?' asked her husband. 'The police or an ambulance?'

My cousin spent heaps on deodorant, until he found out people just didn't like him.

Did you hear about the two bodies
cremated at the same time?

It was a dead heat.

When the fat man was run over by
a steam roller, what was proved?

That he had lots of guts.

Boy: 'Dad there's a black cat
in the dining room!'

Dad: 'That's okay son, black cats are lucky.'

Son: 'This one is – he's eaten your dinner!'

The cruise ship passenger was feeling
really seasick, when the waiter asked
if she'd like some lunch.

'No thanks,' she replied. 'Just throw it over
the side and save me the trouble.'

A mushroom walks into a bar and says
to the bartender, 'Get me a drink!'

But the bartender refuses.

The mushrooms says, 'Why not?
I'm a fun-gi!'

What's the difference between a
peeping Tom and someone who's
just got out of the bath?

One is rude and nosey.
The other is nude and rosey!

She's so ugly, when a wasp stings her,
it has to shut its eyes!

A man out for a walk came across a
little boy pulling his cat's tail.

'Hey you!' he shouted.
'Don't pull the cat's tail!'

'I'm not pulling,' replied the boy. 'I'm only
holding on – the cat's doing the pulling!'

There's no point in telling some people a joke
with a double meaning. They wouldn't
understand either of them!

George is the type of boy that his mother doesn't want him to hang around with.

Three guys, Shutup, Manners and Poop, drove too fast and Poop fell out of the car. Shutup went to the police station, where the policeman asked, 'What's your name?'

'Shutup,' he answered.

'Hey – where are your manners!' the policeman exclaimed.

Shutup replied, 'Outside on the road, scrapin' up Poop!'

My dad once stopped a man
ill-treating a donkey.

It was a case of brotherly love.

Three girls walked into a barber shop.
Two had blonde hair and one had green
hair. The barber asked the blondes,
'How did you get to be blonde?'

'Oh, it's natural,' they replied.

The barber asked the other girl, 'How did
your hair become green?'

*She replied, 'Now put your hand on
your nose and rub up to your hair.'*

Uncle Hubert noticed that his nephew
Johnny was watching him the whole time.

*'Why are you always looking
at me?' he asked.*

'I was just wondering when you were going
to do your trick,' replied Johnny.

'What trick?' asked Uncle Hubert.

'Well, Mum says you drink like a fish . . .'

I don't know what your Mother's on about.
...But slip that drink into my fin
and I'll drink it for you...no worries!

What do you get when you cross
a vampire with a dwarf?

*A monster which sucks blood
out of people's kneecaps.*

The mother monster asked her son what he was doing with a saw, and if he'd seen his brother.

'You mean my new half-brother, Mummy,' he replied!

What goes in pink and comes out blue?

A swimmer on a cold day!

What is the smelliest game in the world?

Ping-Pong!

A woman was facing court, charged with wounding her husband.

'You're very lucky you're not facing a murder charge – why did you stab him over a hundred times?' asked the judge.

'I didn't know how to turn off the electric carving knife,' she replied.

Roger was in a full bus when a fat lady opposite said to him, 'If you were a gentleman, you'd stand up and let someone else sit down.'

'And if you were a lady,' Roger replied, 'you'd stand up and let four people sit down!'

What do you give an elephant with diarrhoea?

Plenty of room.

Did you hear the joke about the fart?

It stinks.

Someone stole all the toilet seats from the police station. The officers have nothing to go on.

Teacher: 'How was your holiday, Penny?'

Penny: 'Great. My brother and I spent
the whole time on the beach, burying
each other in the sand.'

Teacher: 'That sounds like fun.'

Penny: 'Daddy says we can go back next year
and find him.'

What baseball position did the boy
with no arms or legs play?

Home base.

What did the first mate see in the toilet?

The captain's log.

Why are sausages so bad mannered?

They spit in the frying pan.

What do Eskimos get from sitting
on the ice too long?

Polaroids.

Three kids were playing in a park when a genie appeared. The genie said they could have one wish each, so long as they made the wish while coming down the slide. The first kid slid down shouting, 'I want a big glass of lemonade.' The second kid slid down shouting, 'I want a chocolate milkshake.' The third kid slid down shouting, 'Weeeeee.'

What do you call a boy who eats his mother and his father?

An orphan.

What is black and white and red all over?

A nun in a blender.

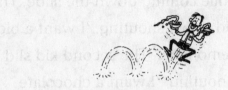

What is twenty metres long
and smells of wee?

Line dancing at the old people's home.

What has four legs and an arm?

A happy lion.

What's green and slimy and
hangs from trees?

Giraffe boogie.

What do you get if you cross an elephant
with a box of laxatives?

Out of the way.

What's green, has two legs and sits
on the end of your finger?

The boogieman.

What's Mozart up to now?

Decomposing.

What's thick and black and picks its nose?

Crude oil.

What's the difference between an oral
thermometer and a rectal thermometer?

The taste.

Where do lepers shop?

At the secondhand store.

Why did the boy take his own toilet
paper to the birthday party?

Because he was a party pooper.

Why do farts smell?

*So that blind people can appreciate
them as well.*

What do you find up a clean nose?

Fingerprints.

Why don't elephants pick their nose?

*Because they don't know what to do
with a 20 kilogram boogie.*

Why was the sailor buried at sea?

Because he was dead.

Woman 1: 'Your son is terribly spoiled.'

Woman 2: *'How dare you. He's not spoiled at all.'*

Woman 1: 'Yes he is. He just got hit by a bus.'

What's invisible and smells of carrots?

Bunny farts!!

Why do gorillas have big nostrils?

Because they have big fingers.

Why did the toilet paper roll down the hill?

To get to the bottom.

Why did the surfer stop surfing?

Because the sea weed.

What is a cannibal's favourite soup?

One with a lot of body.

First Cannibal: 'My girlfriend's
a tough old bird.'

*Second Cannibal: 'You should have left
her in the oven for another half hour.'*

First Cannibal: 'Who was that girl
I saw you with last night?'

*Second Cannibal: 'That was no girl,
that was my dinner.'*

Cannibal 1: 'How do you make
an explorer stew?'

Cannibal 2: 'Keep him waiting a few hours.'

Did you hear about the cannibal who
gnawed a bone for hours on end?

When he stood up, he fell over.

How can you help a hungry cannibal?

Give him a hand.

Mr Cannibal: 'I've brought a friend

home for dinner.'

Mrs Cannibal: 'But I've already made a stew.'

Two cannibals were having lunch.

'Your girlfriend makes a great soup,'

said one to the other.

'Yes!' agreed the first. 'But I'm

going to miss her!'

What did the cannibal say to the explorer?

'Nice to meat you.'

What did the cannibal say when he saw his wife chopping up a python and a pygmy?

'Yum, snake and pygmy pie.'

What did the cannibal say when he saw Dr Livingstone?

'Dr Livingstone, I consume.'

What did the cannibal say when he was full?

'I couldn't eat another mortal.'

What do the guests do at a cannibal wedding?

Toast the bride and groom.

What do vegetarian cannibals eat?

Swedes.

What does a cannibal say when a
bus load of tourists drives past?

'Smorgasbord.'

What's the favourite game at a
cannibal's birthday party?

Swallow the leader.

What was the cannibal called,
who ate her father's sister?

An aunt-eater!

Where do cannibals work?

At head office.

Why did the cannibal eat the missionary?

*Because he'd developed
a taste for Christianity.*

Why did the cannibal kidnap the tourist?

He wanted take-away.

Why did the cannibal live on his own?

He'd had his fill of other people.

Why don't cannibals eat
weather forecasters?

Because they give them wind.

Mummy, Mummy, I don't want
to go to New Zealand.

Shut up and keep swimming.

When the cannibal crossed the Pacific on a cruise ship, he told the waiter to take the menu away and bring him the passenger list!

Mummy, Mummy, Dad has been run over by a steamroller.

Shut up and slide him under the door.

Mummy, Mummy, Daddy's on fire.

Hurry up and get the marshmallows.

Mummy, Mummy, what's a vampire?

Shut up and eat your soup before it clots.

Mummy, Mummy, why do I keep
going round in circles?

*Shut up or I'll nail your
other foot to the floor.*

Mummy, Mummy, are you
sure you bake bread this way?

Shut up and get back in.
I can't close the oven door.

Mummy, Mummy, can I play with Rover?

We've already dug him up
three times this week.

Mummy, Mummy, my head hurts.

Shut up and get away from the dart board.

Mummy, Mummy, Dad's going out.

*Shut up and throw some
more petrol on him.*

Mummy, Mummy, Daddy just
put Rover down.

I'm sure he had a good reason for it.

But he promised I could do it.

Mummy, Mummy, Daddy's hammering
on the roof again.

Shut up and drive a bit faster.

Mummy, Mummy, I can't
find the dog's food.

Shut up and eat your stew.

Mummy, Mummy, I feel like a yo-yo.

Shut up and sit down . . .
and down . . . and down . . .

Mummy, Mummy, I'm 16 years old. Don't
you think I'm old enough to wear a bra now?

Shut up, George.

Mummy, Mummy, I hate my brother's guts.

Shut up and eat what's on your plate.

Mummy, Mummy, sis has got a bruise.

Shut up and eat around it.

Mummy, Mummy, what are
you doing with that ax . . .

Mummy, Mummy, when are we going to
have Grandma for dinner?

*Shut up. We haven't finished
eating your father yet.*

Mummy, Mummy, I've just
chopped my foot off.

*Then hop out of the kitchen,
I've just mopped the floor.*

Mummy, Mummy, why are we
pushing the car off the cliff?

Shut up or you'll wake your father.

Mummy, Mummy, why can't we give
Grandma a proper burial?

Shut up and keep flushing.

Mummy, Mummy, why is
Dad running in zig zags?

Shut up and keep shooting.

Mummy, Mummy, why can't we
buy a garbage disposal unit?

Shut up and keep chewing.

Doctor, Doctor, what is the best
way to avoid biting insects?

Don't bite any.

Doctor, Doctor, I feel like a tennis racket.

You must be too highly strung.

Doctor, Doctor, my nose is running.

You'd better tie it up then.

Doctor, Doctor, I'm afraid of the dark.

Then leave the light on.

Doctor, Doctor, I keep stealing things.

Take one of these pills and if that doesn't work, bring me back a computer.

Doctor, Doctor, I feel like a pair of socks.

Well I'll be darned.

Doctor, Doctor, I have a hoarse throat.

The resemblance doesn't end there.

Doctor, Doctor, I keep thinking I'm a yo-yo.

How are you feeling?

Oh, up and down.

Doctor, Doctor, how can I stop
my nose from running?

Stick your foot out and trip it up.

Doctor, Doctor, people keep
disagreeing with me.

No they don't.

Doctor, Doctor, I'm at death's door.

Don't worry, I'll pull you through.

Doctor, Doctor, my stomach is sore.

Stop your belly aching.

Doctor, Doctor, I'm having trouble breathing.

I'll put a stop to that.

Doctor, Doctor, I keep thinking
I'm a doorknob.

Now don't fly off the handle.

Doctor, Doctor, I'm a wrestler
and I feel awful.

Get a grip on yourself then.

Doctor, Doctor, I think I'm a video.

I thought I'd seen you before.

Doctor, Doctor, I feel like a cricket ball.

How's that?

Oh no, not you too!

Doctor, Doctor, everyone hates me.

Don't be stupid, not everyone
has met you yet.

Doctor, Doctor, I'm suffering
from hallucinations.

I'm sure you are only imagining it.

Doctor, Doctor, will you treat me?

No, you'll have to pay like everybody else.

Doctor, Doctor I keep thinking I'm a $ bill.

Go shopping, the change will do you good.

Doctor, Doctor, I swallowed a spoon.

Well try to relax and don't stir.

Doctor, Doctor, I swallowed a roll of film.

Don't worry, nothing will develop.

Doctor, Doctor, nobody ever listens to me.

Next!

Doctor, Doctor, I'm so ugly what
can I do about it?

Hire yourself out for Halloween parties.

Doctor, Doctor, I feel like a bell.

*Well, take these and if they
don't work, give me a ring.*

Doctor, Doctor, I'm as sick as a dog.

Well, I can't help you because I'm not a vet.

Doctor, Doctor, my eyesight is getting worse.

You're absolutely right, this is a Post Office.

Doctor, Doctor, the first thirty minutes I'm up every morning I feel dizzy, what should I do?

Get up half an hour later.

Doctor, Doctor, what does this
X-Ray of my head show?

Unfortunately nothing.

Doctor, Doctor, this ointment you gave
me makes my arm smart!

Try putting some on your head.

Doctor, Doctor, something is
preying on my mind!

Don't worry, it will probably starve to death.

Doctor, Doctor, I feel like a set of curtains.

Well, pull yourself together.

Doctor, Doctor, I feel run down.

*You should be more careful
crossing the road then.*

Doctor, Doctor, I accidentally ate my doona!

Don't be so down in the mouth.

Doctor, Doctor, I have a ringing in my ears!

Well, answer it.

Doctor, Doctor, every time I stand up I see visions of Mickey Mouse and Pluto and every time I sit down I see Donald Duck!

How long have you been having these Disney spells?

Doctor, Doctor, it hurts when I do this!

Well, don't do that.

Doctor, Doctor, my leg hurts, what can I do?

Limp.

Doctor, Doctor, I snore so loudly
I wake myself up!

Try sleeping in another room.

Doctor, Doctor, everyone thinks I'm a liar.

I don't believe you.

Doctor, Doctor, I have yellow teeth,
what should I do?

Wear a brown tie.

Doctor, Doctor I feel like a dog.

Then go see a vet!

Doctor, Doctor, I have a pain in the eye
every time I drink hot chocolate.

*Take the spoon out of your mug
before you drink.*

Doctor, Doctor, I only have seconds to live!

Just a minute!

Doctor, Doctor, can you help me out?

Certainly – which way did you come in?

Doctor, Doctor, I dreamed that
I ate a large marshmallow!

Did you wake up without a pillow?

Doctor, Doctor, my brother
thinks he's a chicken.

How long has this been going on?

About six months.

Why didn't you bring him here earlier?

We needed the eggs.

Doctor, Doctor, my sister
thinks she's a squirrel.

Sounds like a nut case to me.

Doctor, Doctor, I think I'm getting shorter!

You'll just have to be a little patient.

Doctor Doctor, I keep thinking I'm a dog.

How long has this been going on?

Ever since I was a pup.

Doctor, Doctor, did you hear about
the boy who swallowed a coin?

No? Well, there's no change yet!

Doctor, Doctor, my son swallowed a pen,
what should I do?

Use a pencil instead!

Doctor, Doctor, my wooden leg
is giving me a lot of pain.

Why's that?

My wife keeps hitting me over
the head with it!

Doctor, Doctor, my hair is falling out, can you give me something to keep it in?

Yes, a paper bag.

Doctor, Doctor, I keep thinking I'm a billiard ball.

Well, get back in the queue.

Doctor, Doctor, I've been turned into a hare!

Stop rabbiting on about it.

Doctor, Doctor, I keep thinking I'm a dog.

*Well, get up on this couch
and I'll examine you.*

I can't, I'm not allowed on the furniture.

Doctor, Doctor, my little boy swallowed
a bullet, what should I do?

Well for a start, don't point him at me.

Doctor, Doctor, I feel like a window.

Where's the pane?

Doctor, Doctor, I feel like a piano.

Wait a moment while I make some notes.

Doctor, Doctor will my measles
be better by next Monday?

I don't want to make any rash promises.

Doctor, Doctor, I keep thinking
I'm a fruitcake.

What's got into you?

Flour, raisins and cherries.

Doctor, Doctor, my wife thinks I'm
crazy because I like sausages.

That's ridiculous. I like sausages too.

Good, you should come round and see
my collection some time. I've got
hundreds of them.

Doctor, Doctor, I keep hearing
a ringing in my ears.

Where else did you expect to hear it?

Doctor, Doctor, what's good
for biting fingernails?

Very sharp teeth.

Doctor, Doctor, I have a carrot
growing out of my ear.

Amazing! How could that have happened?

I don't understand it –
I planted cabbages in there!

Doctor, Doctor, I've spent so long at my
computer that I now see double.

Well, walk around with one eye shut.

Doctor, Doctor, can you give me anything for excessive wind?

Sure, here's a kite.

Doctor, Doctor, can I have a bottle of aspirin and a pot of glue?

Why?

Because I've got a splitting headache!

Doctor, Doctor, my little brother thinks he's a computer.

Well, bring him in so I can cure him.

I can't, I need to use him to finish my homework!

Doctor, Doctor, should I surf the Internet
on an empty stomach?

No, you should do it on a computer.

Doctor, Doctor, my girlfriend
thinks she's a duck.

*You'd better bring her
in to see me right away.*

I can't – she's already
flown south for the winter.

Doctor, Doctor, I think
I've been bitten by a vampire.

Drink this glass of water.

Will it make me better?

No, but I'll be able to see if your neck leaks!

Doctor, Doctor, I think I'm a bell.

*Take these, and if they don't help,
give me a ring!*

Doctor, Doctor, the pain is still there.

*I can't find a cause for the pain,
though I think it's due to drinking.*

In that case, I'll come back
when you're sober.

Doctor, Doctor, I have a sore throat.

*Pull your pants down and put your
backside against the window.*

What's that got to do with my sore throat?

Nothing. I just hate my neighbours.

Doctor, Doctor, I was playing a
kazoo and I swallowed it.

Lucky you weren't playing the piano.

Doctor, Doctor, I think I'm a bridge.

What's come over you?

Oh, two cars, a large truck and a bus.

Doctor, Doctor, can I have a second opinion?

Of course, come back tomorrow.

Doctor, Doctor, when I press with my
finger here . . . it hurts, and here . . .
it hurts, and here . . .
and here! What do you
think is wrong with me?

Your finger's broken.

Doctor, Doctor, you have to help me out!

*That's easily done, which way
did you come in?*

Doctor, Doctor, I keep thinking I'm God.

When did this start?

After I created the sun, then the earth . . .

Doctor, Doctor, have you
taken my temperature?

No. Is it missing?

Doctor, Doctor, I feel like a spoon!

Well, sit down and don't stir!

Doctor, Doctor, I keep thinking I'm a joke.

Don't make me laugh.

Doctor, Doctor, I think I need glasses.

You certainly do – you've just walked into a restaurant!

Doctor, Doctor, I've just swallowed a pen.

Well, sit down and write your name!

Doctor, Doctor, I feel like a dog.

Sit!

Doctor, Doctor, I feel like an apple.

We must get to the core of this!

Doctor, Doctor, I feel like a sheep.

That's baaaaaaaaaad!

Doctor, Doctor, I'm becoming invisible.

Yes, I can see you're not all there!

Doctor, Doctor, will this ointment
clear up my spots?

I never make rash promises!

Doctor, Doctor, everyone keeps
throwing me in the garbage.

Don't talk rubbish!

Doctor, Doctor, I'm turning into a dustbin.

Don't talk such rubbish.

Doctor, Doctor, I'm boiling up!

Just simmer down!

Doctor, Doctor, I feel like a needle.

I see your point!

Doctor, Doctor, how can
I cure my sleepwalking?

Sprinkle tin-tacks on your bedroom floor!

Doctor, Doctor, I feel like a racehorse.

Take one of these every four laps!

Doctor, Doctor, I feel like a bee.

Buzz off, I'm busy!

Doctor, Doctor, I'm a burglar!

Have you taken anything for it?

Doctor, Doctor, I keep seeing
an insect spinning.

*Don't worry, it's just a bug
that's going around.*

Doctor, Doctor, I need some acetylsalicylic acid.

You mean aspirin?

That's it. I can never remember that word.

Doctor, Doctor, I feel like an apple.

Well don't worry, I won't bite.

An apple a day didn't keep me away from the doctor's

Doctor, Doctor, my tongue tingles when
I touch it to an unsalted peanut wrapped
in used toaster oven aluminium foil.
What's wrong with me?

You have far too much free time.

Doctor, Doctor, I tend to flush a lot.

Don't worry, it's just a chain reaction.

Doctor, Doctor, everyone thinks I'm a liar.

Well, that's hard to believe!

Doctor, Doctor, I think I'm a python.

*You can't get round me
just like that, you know!*

Doctor, Doctor, I think I'm a moth.

So why did you come around then?

Well, I saw this light at the window . . .

Doctor, Doctor, I keep thinking I'm a spider.

What a web of lies!

Doctor, Doctor, I think I'm a snail.

*Don't worry, we'll soon have
you out of your shell.*

Doctor, Doctor, I think I'm an adder.

*Great, can you help me with
my accounts then please?*

Doctor, Doctor, I keep painting myself gold.

Don't worry, it's just a gilt complex.

Doctor, Doctor, my baby looks
just like his father.

Never mind – just as long as he's healthy.

Doctor, Doctor, everyone keeps ignoring me.

Next please!

Doctor, Doctor, I keep thinking
I'm a computer.

*My goodness, you'd better come to my
surgery right away!*

I can't, my power cable won't reach that far!

Doctor, Doctor, I don't think I'm a computer
any more. Now I think I'm a desk.

You're just letting things get on top of you.

Doctor, Doctor, I keep thinking
there's two of me.

One at a time please!

Doctor, Doctor, some days I feel like a
tee-pee and other days I feel like a wigwam.

You're too tents!

Doctor, Doctor, my little boy has just
swallowed a roll of film.

Hmmm. Let's hope nothing develops!

Doctor, Doctor, I feel like a pack of cards.

I'll deal with you later!

Doctor, Doctor, how much to have
this splinter pulled out?

Seventy dollars.

Seventy dollars for just a
couple of minutes' work?

I can pull it out very slowly if you like.

Doctor, Doctor, I snore so loud that
I keep myself awake.

Sleep in another room, then.

Doctor, Doctor, I think I'm a yo-yo.

You're stringing me along!

Doctor, Doctor, I keep thinking
I'm a vampire.

Necks, please!

Doctor, Doctor, I swallowed a bone.

Are you choking?

No, I really did!

Doctor, Doctor, I dream there are zombies
under my bed. What can I do?

Saw the legs off your bed.

Doctor, Doctor, I think I'm a woodworm.

How boring for you!

Doctor, Doctor, I think I'm an electric eel.

That's shocking!

Doctor, Doctor, I think I'm a nit.

Will you get out of my hair?

Doctor, Doctor, I keep thinking
I'm a mosquito.

Go away, sucker!

Doctor, Doctor, I've broken
my arm in two places.

Well, don't go back there again.

Doctor, Doctor, I think I'm a butterfly.

*Will you say what you mean
and stop flitting about!*

Doctor, Doctor, I think I'm a frog.

What's wrong with that?

I think I'm going to croak!

Doctor, Doctor, I think I'm a caterpillar.

Don't worry, you'll soon change.

Doctor, Doctor, I think I'm a snake,
about to shed its skin.

*Why don't you go behind the screen and slip
into something more comfortable, then!*

Doctor, Doctor, these pills you
gave me for B.O. . .

What's wrong with them?

They keep slipping out from under my arms!

Doctor, Doctor, my husband
smells like a fish.

Poor sole!

Doctor, Doctor, my sister thinks she's a lift.

Well, tell her to come in.

I can't, she doesn't stop at this floor!

Doctor, Doctor, I think I'm a moth.

Get out of the way, you're in my light!

Doctor, Doctor, how long have I got?

Ten.

Ten what? Ten months? Ten weeks?

10, 9, 8, 7 . . .

Doctor, Doctor, how was my check up?

Perfect. You'll live to be 80.

But I am 80.

In that case, it's been nice knowing you.

Doctor, Doctor, have you got
something for a migraine?

*Take this hammer and hit
yourself on the head.*

Doctor, Doctor, I ate some oysters
and now I'm feeling sick.

Were they fresh?

How can you tell?

You open the shell and have a look.

You're not supposed to eat the shell?

Doctor, Doctor, I came as quick as
I could. What's the problem?

*Your lab results are back and you've
only got 24 hours to live.*

That's terrible.

*There's worse. I've been trying
to call you since yesterday.*

Doctor, Doctor, I get very nervous and
frightened during driving tests.

Don't worry, you'll pass eventually.

But I'm the examiner!

Doctor, Doctor, I can't feel my legs.

That's because we had to amputate your arms.

Doctor, Doctor, I feel like a bird.

I'll tweet you in a minute.

Doctor, Doctor, I feel like a strawberry.

I can see you're in a bit of a jam.

Doctor, Doctor, I think I'm a rubber band.

Why don't you stretch yourself out on the couch there, and tell me all about it?

Doctor, Doctor, I keep seeing double.

Please sit on the couch.

Which one?

Doctor, Doctor, I keep seeing green aliens with two heads and four legs.

Have you seen a psychiatrist?

No, just green aliens with two heads and four legs.

Doctor, Doctor, I keep thinking I'm a bee.

Buzz off, I'm busy.

Doctor, Doctor, my wife keeps beating me.

Oh dear. How often?

Every time we play Scrabble.

Doctor, Doctor, I need something
for my temper.

Just wait 'til you get the bill.

Doctor, Doctor, I swallowed
a whole cantaloupe.

You're just feeling melon-choly.

Doctor, Doctor, I feel like a pair of curtains.

Oh, pull yourself together!

Doctor, Doctor, I think I'm a clock.

You're winding me up.

Doctor, Doctor, I think I'm invisible.

Come back later. I can't see you now.

Doctor, Doctor, I think I'm losing my mind.

Don't worry, you won't miss it.

Doctor, Doctor, I think I'm turning into a woman.

Well, you are 16 now Amanda.

Doctor, Doctor, I think I'm suffering from déjà vu.

Haven't I seen you before?

Doctor, Doctor, I've got a terrible cold. What should I do?

Go home, take a hot bath then stand outside in the cold with no clothes on.

But if I do that, I'll get pneumonia.

That's the idea. I can treat pneumonia. I can't treat a cold.

Doctor, Doctor, I've lost my memory.

When did this happen?

When did what happen?

Doctor, Doctor, if I give up wine, women and song, will I live longer?

No, but it will seem longer.

Doctor, Doctor, I've got jelly in my ear.

You're just a trifle deaf.

Doctor, Doctor, I think I'm a computer.

How long have you felt like this?

Ever since I was switched on!

Doctor, Doctor, my baby's swallowed some explosives.

Well, don't annoy him. We don't want him to go off.

Doctor, Doctor, my hands
won't stop shaking.

Do you drink a lot?

No, most of it spills.

Doctor, Doctor, my son swallowed
my razor-blade.

Well, just use your electric razor.

Doctor, Doctor, my wife's contractions
are only five minutes apart.

Is this her first child?

No, this is her husband.

Doctor, Doctor, should I file my nails?

No, throw them away like everyone else does.

Doctor, Doctor, since the operation
on my leg, I lean one way.

I think you're all right.

Doctor, Doctor, sometimes I feel like a goat.

How long has this been going on?

Ever since I was a kid.

Doctor, Doctor, I can't get to sleep.

*Sit on the edge of the bed and
you'll soon drop off.*

Doctor, Doctor, sometimes I feel like an onion
and sometimes I feel like a cucumber.

You've got yourself in a bit of a pickle.

Doctor, Doctor, sometimes
I think I'm a biscuit.

You're crackers.

Doctor, Doctor, sometimes I think
there are two of me.

Good, you can pay both bills on the way out.

Doctor, Doctor, tell me straight. Is it bad?

Just don't start watching any new TV serials.

Doctor, Doctor, what's wrong with me?

Well, you've got a carrot up your nose, a bean in one ear and a French fry in the other. I'd say you're not eating properly.

Doctor, Doctor, will I be able to play the violin when my hand heals?

Of course.

Great. Because I couldn't play it before.

Doctor, Doctor, you've taken out my tonsils, my appendix, my gall bladder and one of my kidneys but I still feel sick.

That's enough out of you.

Doctor, Doctor, I keep seeing spots.

Have you seen an optometrist?

No, just spots.

Doctor, Doctor, I've a split personality.

Well, you'd better both sit down, then.

Doctor, Doctor, my sister keeps
thinking she's invisible.

Which sister?

Waiter, what kind of soup is this?

Bean soup.

I don't care what it's been. What is it now?

Waiter, there's a fly in my soup!

*Don't worry sir, the spider
in your salad will get it!*

Waiter, I'm in a hurry. Will my pizza be long?

No, it will be round.

Waiter, this soup tastes funny.

Why aren't you laughing then?

Waiter, this egg is bad.

Well don't blame me, I only laid the table.

Waiter, there's a bug in my soup.

Be quiet, sir or everyone will want one.

Waiter, how long will my sausages be?

Oh, about eight centimetres.

Waiter, you've got your thumb on my steak!

Well I didn't want to drop it again.

If I don't
it will slide
off with
everything
else

Waiter, there's a fly in my soup.

Yes sir, the hot water killed it.

Waiter, how did this fly get in my soup?

I guess it flew.

Waiter, I can't eat this meal.
Fetch me the manager.

It's no use. He won't eat it either.

Waiter, do you have frogs' legs?

Yes sir.

Then hop to the kitchen and fetch me a steak.

Waiter, I'd like burnt steak and soggy
chips with a grimy, bitter salad.

I'm afraid the chef won't cook that for you, sir.

Why not? He did yesterday.

Waiter, I'll have the burger please.

With pleasure.

No, with fries.

Waiter, I'll have the lamb chops.
And make them lean.

Certainly sir. To the right or the left?

Waiter, what is this fly doing in my soup?

Freestyle I believe.

Waiter, I'll have the soup and the fish please.

I would recommend you eat the fish first.
It's been sitting around for a few days
and is starting to pong.

Waiter, is there any soup on the menu?

No madam, I've wiped it all off.

Waiter, is this beef or lamb?

Can't you taste the difference?

No.

Then it doesn't matter.

Waiter, remove this fly now.

But he hasn't finished yet.

Waiter, there's a cockroach in my soup.

Sorry sir, we're all out of flies.

Waiter, there's a dead fly
swimming in my soup.

There can't be, sir. Dead flies can't swim.

Waiter, there's a flea in my soup.

Tell him to hop it.

Waiter, do you serve crabs
in this restaurant?

Yes sir, we serve anyone.

Waiter, there's a fly in my soup.

*I find that hard to believe, sir. The chef
used them all in the casserole.*

Waiter, there's a fly in my soup.

*No sir, that's a cockroach.
The fly's on your roll.*

Waiter, there's a fly in my soup.

That's because the chef used to be a tailor.

Waiter, there's a fly in my soup.

Would you prefer him in your main course?

Waiter, there's a fly on my steak.

That's because it's attracted to rotting meat.

Waiter, there's a spider in my soup.

It must have eaten the fly.

Waiter, this apple pie is squashed.

Well, you told me to step on it
because you were in a hurry.

Waiter, this crab has only got one claw.
It must have been in a fight.

Then bring me the winner.

Waiter, this coffee tastes like mud.

I can't understand why. It was ground just a minute ago.

Waiter, we'll have two coffees please. And I want a clean cup.

Yes, sir. Here are your two coffees. Now which one of you wanted the clean cup?

Waiter, what do you call this dish?

Chicken surprise.

But I can't see any chicken?

That's the surprise.

Waiter, what's this in my soup?

I don't know, sir. All bugs look the same to me.

Waiter, do you have frogs' legs?

No, I've always walked like this.

Waiter, there is a small insect in my soup!

Sorry sir, I'll get you a bigger one!

What do you call

. . . **a** man who likes to work out?

Jim!

. . . **a** boy with really short hair?

Sean!

. . . **a** woman with a cat on her head?

Kitty!

. . . **a** woman with one leg?

Eileen!

. . . **a** boy hanging on the wall?

Art!

. . . **a** man with a number plate on his head?

Reg!

. . . **a** man with a spade?

Doug!

. . . **a** man without a spade?

Douglas!

. . . a man with a car on his head?

Jack!

. . . a man who owes money?

Bill!

. . . a man in a pile of leaves?

Russell!

. . . a woman in the distance?

Dot!

. . . Someone who greets you at the school door every morning?

Matt!

. . . a man with a plank on his head?

Edward!

. . . a man with a paper bag on his head?

Russell!

. . . a girl with a frog on her head?

Lily!

. . . **a** man with a seagull on his head?

Cliff!

. . . **a** man with a crane on his head?

Derek!

. . . **a** man with a wig on his head?

Aaron!

. . . **a** man with a mat on his head?

Neil!

. . . **a** woman with a radiator on her head?

Anita!

. . . **a** woman with slates on her head?

Ruth!

. . . **a** man with a large black and blue mark on his head?

Bruce!

. . . **a** man with some cat scratches on his head?

Claude!

. . . a man with a map on his head?

Miles!

. . . a man with a stamp on his head?

Frank!

. . . a woman with a toilet on her head?

Lu!

. . . a woman with two toilets on her head?

Lulu!

. . . a woman with a breeze on her head?

Gail!

. . . a woman with a tortoise on her head?

Shelley!

. . . a woman with a twig on her head?

Hazel!

. . . a man with a kilt on his head?

Scott!

. . . a man with a legal document
on his head?

Will!

. . . a woman with a Christmas
tree on her head?

Carol!

. . . a man with a Christmas
tree on his head?

Noel!

. . . **a** man with a truck on his head?

The deceased!

. . . **a** boy who is always
getting up your nose?

Vic!

. . . **a** girl with one foot on
each side of a river?

Bridget!

. . . **a** man floating in the sea?

Bob!

. . . a man who drives a truck?

Laurie!

. . . a Russian gardener?

Ivanhoe!

. . . a lady standing in the middle
of a tennis court?

Annette!

. . . a woman who can balance a
bottle of beer on her head?

Beatrix!

. . . **a** woman who gambles?

Betty!

. . . **a** man with beef, gravy and vegetables on his head?

Stu!

. . . **a** German barber?

Herr Dresser!

. . . **a** man sitting in a tree?

Woody!

. . . **a** woman who climbs up walls?

Ivy!

. . . **a** man with rabbits in his trousers?

Warren!

. . . **a** man who is always around
when you need him?

Andy!

What will Bob the Builder be
called when he retires?

Bob.

Person 1: 'Why are you wearing garlic
around your neck?'

Person 2: 'It keeps away vampires.'

Person 1: 'But there are no vampires.'

Person 2: 'See, it works.'

A ghost walks into a bar.

*Bartender: 'Sorry, we don't
serve spirits here.'*

Did you hear about the ghosts' running race?

It was a dead heat.

Did you hear about the vampire comedian?

He specialised in biting satire.

Did you hear about the vampire who got taken away in a straightjacket?

He went batty.

Did you hear about the weather wizard?

He's forecasting sunny spells.

Do zombies like the dark?

Of corpse they do.

How can you tell if a corpse is angry?

It flips its lid.

What do you get if you cross a
dinosaur with a vampire?

A blood shortage.

How can you tell what a ghost
is getting for its birthday?

By feeling its presence.

How do you greet a three-headed monster?

'Hello, hello, hello.'

How do you greet a six-headed monster?

'I didn't know you were twins.'

How do you make a witch itch?

Take away the 'W'.

How does a yeti feel when it gets a cold?

Abominable.

How does Dracula eat his food?

In bite sized pieces.

Police Officer 1: 'Where's the skeleton?'

Police Officer 2: 'I had to let him go.'

Police Officer 1: 'But he's our main suspect.'

*Police Officer 2: 'I know.
But I couldn't pin anything on him.'*

What did Frankenstein do when he saw the monster catcher approaching?

He bolted.

What is Dracula's favourite fruit?

Necktarines!

What did Quasimodo become after he died?

A dead ringer.

What did the alien say to her son
when he returned home?

'Where on Earth have you been?'

What did the alien say to the plant?

'Take me to your weeder.'

What did the ghost buy for his wife?

A see-through nightie.

What did the sea monster say when it saw the brand new ocean liner sail past?

'Yum. Launch time.'

What do goblin children do after school?

Their gnomework.

What do little zombies play?

Corpses and robbers.

What do monsters have mid-morning?

A coffin break.

Why doesn't anyone kiss vampires?

Because they have bat breath.

What do sea monsters eat?

Fish and ships.

What do vampire footballers
have at half times?

Blood oranges.

What do you call a twelve-foot,
two-headed monster?

Anything it likes.

What do you call a detective skeleton?

Sherlock Bones.

What do you call a ghost's mum and dad?

Transparents.

What do you call a hairy beast in a river?

A weir-wolf.

What do you call a protest march by devils?

A demon-stration.

What do you call a skeleton who
sits around doing nothing?

Lazy bones.

What does a monster say when introduced?

'Pleased to eat you.'

What do you call a witch
without a broomstick?

A witch-hiker.

What do you do if you're surrounded
by a witch, a werewolf, a vampire
and two ghosts?

Hope you're at a fancy dress party.

What do zombies use to make cakes?

Self-raising flour.

What does a monster call his parents?

Dead and mummy.

What does a vampire never
order at a restaurant?

Stake.

What does an undertaker
take before starting work?

A stiff drink.

What does a devil do to keep fit?

Exorcise.

What happened to the naughty
schoolgirl witch?

She was ex-spelled.

What did the witch say to the vampire?

'Get a life!'

What happened when the
gravediggers went on strike?

Their job was done by a skeleton crew.

What is a vampire's favourite sport?

Batminton.

What is a witch's favourite movie?

'Broom with a View.'

What is Dr Jekyll's favourite game?

Hyde and seek.

What is Dracula's car called?

A mobile blood unit.

What is the favourite fun fair
ride for little ghosts?

The rollerghoster.

What is the first part of a newspaper
that a ghost turns to?

The horror-scope.

What kind of plate does a skeleton eat off?

Bone china.

What kind of cheese do monsters eat?

Monsterella!

What song did the band play at the Demons and Ghouls ball?

'Demons are a Ghoul's Best Friend.'

What trees do ghosts like best?

Ceme-trees.

What type of music do mummies like best?

Ragtime.

What type of music do zombies like best?

Soul music.

What vehicles race at the Witches'
Formula One Grand Prix?

Vroomsticks.

What was the skeleton rock band called?

The Strolling Bones.

What was the wizard's favourite band?

ABBA-cadabra.

What's a vampire's favourite dance?

The fangdango.

What don't zombies wear on boat trips?

Life jackets.

What's three metres tall, has twelve fingers
and three eyes and wears sunglasses?

A monster on its summer holiday.

What's a skeleton's favourite
musical instrument?

A trom-bone.

Where do Australian ghosts live?

In the Northern Terror-tory.

Where do ghosts go swimming?

In the Dead Sea.

Which ghost is President of France?

Charles de Ghoul.

Which ghost ate the three bears' porridge?

Ghouldilocks.

Who did the witch call when
her broom was stolen?

The flying squad.

Who finished last at the Yeti Olympics?

Frosty the Slowman.

Why did Dracula take some medicine?

To stop his coffin.

Who is big and hairy, wears a dress and climbs the Empire State Building?

Queen Kong.

Who is King of the Cannibals?

Henry the Ate.

Who is the King of the Wizards?

William the Conjurer.

Who won the running race between Count Dracula and Countess Dracula?

It was neck and neck.

Why are Cyclops couples happy together?

Because they always see eye to eye.

Why are ghosts always tired?

Because they are dead on their feet.

Why couldn't the witch race her
horse in the Witches' Derby?

Because it was having a spell.

Why did the demon jump into the conserve?

Because he was a jammy devil.

Why do witches fly on broomsticks?
Because it's better than walking.

Why did the witches go on strike?
Because they wanted sweeping reforms.

Why did the executioner go to work early?

To get a head start.

Why did the vampire go to the orthodontist?

To improve his bite.

Why did the young vampire follow
his dad's profession?

Because it was in his blood.

Why didn't the skeleton bother
to defend itself in court?

Because it didn't have a leg to stand on.

Why didn't the skeleton want to go to work?

Because his heart wasn't in it.

Why do ghosts like the Spice Girls?

Because they're an all ghoul band.

Why do ghosts speak Latin?

Because it's a dead language.

Why did the zombie decide
to stay in his coffin?

He felt rotten.

Why do skeletons drink milk?

Because it's good for the bones.

Why do skeletons hate winter?

*Because the wind just goes
straight through them.*

Why do vampires play poker?

Because they like playing for high stakes.

Why do witches get good bargains?

Because they're good at haggling.

Why don't ghosts bother telling lies?

Because you can see right through them.

Why is Count Dracula skinny?

Because he eats necks to nothing.

Why isn't the Abominable Snowman
scared of people?

Because he doesn't believe in them.

What do vampires cross the sea in?

Blood vessels.

What did King Kong say when
his sister had a baby?

Well I'll be a monkey's uncle.

What's green, sits in the corner and cries?

The Incredible Sulk.

What happened when the
Abominable Snowman ate a curry?

He melted.

What do you call a good looking, kind and
considerate monster?

A complete failure.

What do sea monsters eat for lunch?

Potato ships!

Why did the cyclops give up teaching?

Because he only had one pupil.

What do devils drink?

Demonade.

What do you call a sleeping monster
who won't keep quiet?

Frankensnore.

What happened to Frankenstein's monster
when he was caught speeding?

*He was fined $50 and dismantled
for six months.*

What's a vampire's favourite dog?

A bloodhound!

What happened to the monster that took
the five o'clock train home?

He had to give it back.

What do you get when you cross a
vampire and a snowman?

Frostbite!

What do you get when you cross
a skunk with Frankenstein?

Stinkenstein!

What did the baby zombie
want for his birthday?

A deady bear.

What did the vampire say when
he had bitten someone?

'It's been nice gnawing you!'

What do you do with a green monster?

Put him in a paper bag till he ripens.

What is Dracula's favourite
ice cream flavour?

Vein-illa!

Why didn't the skeleton cross the road?

Because he didn't have the guts to!

What did the alien say to the petrol pump?

*Take your finger out of your ear
when I'm talking to you.*

What do you call a lamb
with a machine gun?

Lambo.

Why don't turkeys get invited
to dinner parties?

Because they use fowl language.

What do you get when you cross
a rooster with a steer?

A cock and bull story.

Why did the lizard cross the road?

To see his flat mate.

What do you call an elephant
that never washes?

A smellyphant.

What do you get if you cross
a skunk with a bear?

Winnie the Poo.

What swings through the trees
and is very dangerous?

A chimpanzee with a machine-gun.

How did the skunk phone his mother?

On a smellular phone.

What do frogs order in restaurants?

French Flies!

What's worse than finding a
worm in your apple?

Finding half a worm!

What's white on the outside,
green on the inside and hops?

A frog sandwich.

What do you call a group of people
that dig for bones?

A skeleton crew.

What did the floor say to the desk?

I can see your drawers.

What's brown and sticky?

A stick.

What's the hardest part about sky diving?

The ground!

Why didn't the man die
when he drank poison?

Because he was in the living room.

What do you get if you pour
hot water down a rabbit hole?

Hot cross bunnies.

Why did the one-handed
man cross the road?

He wanted to get to the second-hand shop!

What's a lion's favourite food?

Baked beings.

Boy monster: 'You've got a
face like a million dollars.'

Girl monster: 'Have I really?'

Boy monster: 'Sure, it's green and wrinkly!'

First Boy: 'Does your brother keep himself clean?'

Second Boy: *'Oh, yes, he takes a bath every month, whether he needs one or not!'*

Mum: 'Haven't you finished filling the salt shaker yet?'

Son: *'Not yet. It's really hard to get the salt through all those little holes!'*

John: 'Have you noticed your mother smells a bit funny these days?'

Will: *'No. Why?'*

John: 'Well, your sister told me she was giving her a bottle of toilet water for her birthday!'

How did the dentist become
a brain surgeon?

His drill slipped.

What did the undertaker say to his
girlfriend?

'Em-balmy about you!'

What has four wheels and flies?

A garbage truck.

How do you make a Venetian blind?

Poke his eyes out.

Person 1: 'Pssst. Do you want to buy the genuine skull of Julius Caesar?'

Person 2: 'You sold me his skull last week. Besides, that one is smaller.'

Person 1: 'This is when he was a boy.'

Person 1: 'I've never been so insulted in all my life.'

Person 2: 'You haven't been trying.'

'That dress fits you like a glove. It sticks out in five places.'

The guy who invented the hokey pokey died but they couldn't get him into the coffin. His right leg was in, then his right leg was out, his right leg was . . .

When do you put a frog in your sister's bed?

When you can't find a mouse.

What happens when the Queen burps?

She issues a royal pardon.

What do you call a man with an elephant on his head?

Squashed.

What's the nearest thing to silver?

The Lone Ranger's bottom.

What did one toilet say to the other toilet?

'You look a bit flushed!'

I have five noses, seven ears and four mouths. What am I?

Very ugly.

What did one eye say to the other eye?

'Something that smells has come between us.'